# THE GEORGE FOSTER STORY

# THE GEORGE FOSTER STORY

by MALKA DRUCKER
with GEORGE FOSTER

Introduction by George Foster

Holiday House, New York

Grateful acknowledgment is made to the following: the people who spoke about George Foster, especially his sister and mother; the Reds and Dodgers for their cooperation; Bill Waller, Jr.; and John Briggs.


Printed in the United States of America

*Library of Congress Cataloging in Publication Data*

Drucker, Malka.
The George Foster story.

Includes index.
SUMMARY: A biography of one of the few National League baseball players to hit over 50 home runs in a single season.
1. Foster, George, 1948 (Dec. 1)-
—Juvenile literature. 2. Baseball players—
United States—Biography—Juvenile literature.
[1. Foster, George, 1948 (Dec. 1)- 2. Baseball players. 3. Afro-Americans—Biography]
I. Foster, George, 1948 (Dec. 1)- —joint author. II. Title.
GV865.F62D78 796.357'092'4 [B] [92]
ISBN 0-8234-0351-3 78-20616

FOR S.D. WITH LOVE

M.D.

TO GOD WHO DWELLS IN EVERYONE,
TO MY MOTHER, REGINA, WHO IS VERY DEAR TO ME,
TO THE CHILDREN OF THE WORLD

G.F.

# Contents

# List of Photos

PAGE

# THE GEORGE FOSTER STORY

# Introduction

Baseball is only a small but important part of my life. I know that I will not play the game forever, but while I am still in it I will strive to do my best at all times.

Playing baseball is like a dream come true for me. I had always hoped and prayed to get a chance to play in the major leagues. Later I realized that an effort was also needed. Having dreams is good but having them materialize into reality is what's important.

In life I feel that everyone has a purpose. It might take many years of searching, but the important thing is not to give up. Keep on pushing. Go that extra mile. I was blessed to find my interest or purpose in life at a very young age. I had in my mind then that I wanted to play baseball. In growing up, I was fortunate to be able to do and have whatever I needed.

We were not rich, but we had enough to make ends meet.

I was a lot smaller in size, but not in heart, than kids my age. I also had the dedication, confidence, application, and determination to pursue my purpose. And having people who would take time to give me sound advice and words of encouragement along the way helped a lot.

In doing anything worthwhile in life, you need to employ certain ingredients. First, you need to have confidence in yourself. You have to believe you can do something and do it well. You will have setbacks and disappointments and get discouraged on the way, but do not quit, that is if you want to succeed. Yet don't be afraid to fail. One may not recognize that what looks like failure may, in the long run, prove beneficial. Also, success should be measured not so much by the position that one has reached in life as by the obstacles which he has overcome while trying to succeed.

Second, you have to be disciplined. You need to sort out and decide what you need to do and not do with regard to not only your career but also your life. You will have to make sacrifices along the way. Remember that for you to get something worthwhile you have to give something in return.

Third, you have to have patience. It is going to take time and hard work to achieve goals. It will take longer for some than for others. Just don't get impatient. Things will happen in time.

Last but not the least you need faith. You need to have faith in something or someone. I believe in God. He is my strength. But remember to keep your faith in whatever it is when things are going good as well as bad. Faith must be lived every moment of your life. In life every great enterprise begins with and takes its first step forward in faith.

Whatever you strive to do in life, you will be successful in some way, shape, or form. But remember to regard the rights of others and to help someone else make it too. Having worthy goals and purposes in life helps both others and yourself. When you enrich the lives of others, you find your own greater fulfillment. Just find out what you can do and do it to the best of your ability. You are not in competition with others. Use your talents, your gifts, your abilities, and your training to make yourself the best that you can be.

Never lose sight of the important truth that no one can be truly great until he has gained a knowledge of himself. So know yourself and improve yourself. Give a little when things get tough but never stop trying. You get out of life exactly what you put into it. Think positively about yourself. Most of all, be yourself.

As long as you try, you have achieved something.

Don't give up no matter how hopeless it looks. Have faith. If you keep trying, you may wake up one day and find that your dream has become reality.

GEORGE FOSTER

# 1

# The Red Glove

George Arthur Foster sat patiently on the steps outside his house in Tuscaloosa, Alabama, and watched John and Mamie, his big brother and sister, play catch in the hot summer sun. He didn't bother to ask if he could play, because he already knew the answer. "No, you'll get hurt," fifteen-year-old Mamie would say, but George knew better. He was only six, but he'd watched them enough times to know he could do it if given the chance.

He grew bored and got up and walked with a little rubber ball to the cotton fields near his house. The fields looked pretty from a distance, with tight little tufts of white brightening the landscape, but they still made George shudder because, like many black children in the South, he had already learned to pick cotton.

The first morning his mother had sent him to join

his brother and sister in the field, the boss had given him a large sack and had told him to fill it with bits of cotton. At first George found the novelty of the task fun, but he soon grew tired and longed to play. He had to go on picking, though, until he heard the whistle blow to signal the day's end. Struggling to the weighing station with his heavy sack, he was glad to be finished. He hated the job, but had picked so much cotton he was sure he'd be paid well. The weigher grabbed the sack from him and flung it on the scales. The needle jumped to eighty-seven pounds, more than twice George's weight. That was a lot of cotton! But when George held out his hand to be paid, he was given only eighty seven cents, a penny a pound, for a full day's work.

Now he looked away from the cotton and began to throw the ball as hard as he could, high into the air over and over, trying to hit the sky. "I never did hit the sky," he said years later, "but I remember thinking that one day I'd be strong enough to reach it."

It was 1954, and he dreamed that he was Willie Mays, the great New York Giant centerfielder, who had grown up in nearby Westfield, Alabama. Any baseball talk he'd ever heard always included a proud mention of Willie and his accomplishments. Willie was at the peak of his dazzling career and New York sportswriters had run out of adjectives to describe his amazing glove and bat.

George didn't understand yet what baseball really was, except that you needed a bat and ball. But he did know that even if he weren't sure of what Willie Mays actually did, he wanted to grow up and be like this man everyone talked about. Although life in the rural, mostly black community was warm and closely knit, the conversations, mixed with envy and admiration about Willie Mays, hinted that the great ballplayer was living a far better life away from Alabama.

As the old bus bumped along the road that passed through miles of cotton fields, George leaned against his mother and tried to imagine what California would be like. He'd heard stories of blue skies, year-round sunshine, and orange groves. His parents had separated and his mother was taking him, along with John and Mamie, to Southern California. Looking back George said, "I remember really enjoying the trip west, seeing the country, but I was disappointed when we arrived at Hawthorne, California, because it wasn't all they said it was." There were no orange groves in Hawthorne, in fact there were hardly any trees at all. The land was flat like Tuscaloosa, but compared to the open green farm country of the South, Hawthorne was crammed with houses and gas stations. It was also noisy with cars and people, and George, who had always been a quiet boy, became shy from being around so many people all the time.

What made him feel even more self-conscious,

though, was that for the first time in his life he felt different because he was black. He'd never paid much attention to color before, but in California he felt as though he stood out like a sore thumb. He'd had little to do with the white people he saw in Alabama, and he'd gone to an all-black school. When he was born on December 1, 1948, Alabama was still segregated.

As a grown man he remembered his first class in Hawthorne: "I was enrolled in Roosevelt Elementary. I was the only black in the class. It was really something new and very strange to me because I'd never attended school with whites before. In fact we rarely saw white people except for the police and other people in authority."

His shyness grew as the children in his new class stared at him with curiosity. Although he knew that people were all the same no matter what their color, the stares hurt him and he wanted to disappear. Sad and lonely, he rarely spoke unless he had to, and kept to himself.

His teachers would have been surprised to know the anguish behind George's polite face, because he was "the perfect student." He did his work, got good grades, and gave no one any problems. They used him as an example for the other kids, and that cut him off further from making friends.

Fortunately his mother, with her strength and optimism, helped him survive the difficult adjustment to California and integrated society without suffering scars of bitterness. She had to clean houses to support her family, but she found time to teach her children to believe that everything works out for the best, and from this George learned courage and patience. "Looking back," he said later, "I'm glad I became aware about color, because it made me more sensitive about people. If you're with blacks all the time you become one-sided."

He became friends with a quiet Indian boy named Eugene, who loved baseball almost as much as George. From what they had picked up watching the neighborhood softball games, they played their version of baseball together.

One day Eugene came over to George's house with his hands behind his back and a mysterious grin. He was hiding his surprise, an old baseball glove for his friend. George took it shyly and looked at it for a long time. His own glove at last. With all its cracks and missing strings, it was the most beautiful thing he'd ever seen.

"It was my prized possession," George recalled. "I got some red paint and tried to restore some of the color, and some shoelaces to replace the broken strings. Every night I would oil it, put a ball in the pocket and put the glove in the closet."

By the time George was twelve he wanted to play

organized baseball, but the neighborhood people rarely let him play because he was so small and thin. The frustration of watching them play and feeling "any game someone else could play I could play" drove him to find his own team. George never forgot how he got on his first team: "I found a field where other twelve-year-olds were playing ball, and every day I would go over there with my glove and shoes and wait to be asked to play. All the kids wore uniforms. I went back four or five times, waiting to be chosen, but I never was because they always seemed to have enough players. I was never going to go back, but then I learned that this was an organized Little League team and you had to sign up to play."

The next day he went to Larson Field and in a voice just a notch above a whisper asked the coach, John Olson, if he could try out. Olson said that all he had to do was hit the ball and run to first base, and he'd make the team. Excited and nervous, George wasn't sure what the coach had said by the time he had his turn at bat. His shyness kept him from asking anyone what to do, but he felt confident enough to prove that he could play.

Clutching his bat tightly, he took his stance at the plate, ready to hit anything he could reach. He swung hard at the first pitch and felt the wood vibrate in his hands. Without looking or stopping he ran blindly to first, and then because he wasn't sure of the coach's instructions, raced around all the bases. "I guess people thought I was overdoing it," he recalled later, "but I didn't want to take any chances on messing up." As he crossed home plate and saw the coach laugh, he knew immediately he'd made a mistake. He was too embarrassed to ask if he'd made the team, but Olson assured him he was on the roster of the Tri-Park Braves.

*George (third from right, front row) with his first team, the Tri-Park Braves, in 1961. Coach John Olson is in the back row on the left.*

The crisp white and maroon uniform with its maroon cap fit his slender body loosely, but he felt as big as Willie Mays. He would have slept in the uniform and gone to school in it if he had been allowed, because in uniform he felt he was somebody—he was a ballplayer. His mother kept the uniform so immaculate, he recalled, "Even then I hated to slide because my uniform was so clean."

He went to his first game without his family there, but that was all right because he knew he didn't need his mother to do a good job. To play on a team, to be counted on to help others, that's why he wanted to be a Brave, not just to win praise from his family. And George had another important reason for wanting to play on this almost all-white team. "Being black gave me the incentive to show white players how good I was," he said later.

Larson Field wasn't Candlestick Park, but it was nice enough, with wooden fences, a hot dog stand, and lots of seats for the fans. The black minor leagues in the South didn't have parks as comfortable, and it thrilled George to be at Larson.

When it was his first turn at bat, all he could think of was Willie Mays. By now his hero was a legend renowned for his game-saving catches and home runs. George took a wide stance and placed his hands low on the bat, just like Willie. "Give me something to hit," he asked the pitcher silently. The

*George shows his batting stance as a Tri-Park Brave at Larson Field, 1961.*

pitch was released, and he swung so hard he nearly fell over. Strike one. The next pitch he fouled back. He tried to check his swing at the next pitch. "Strike three," the umpire called. George was sure he hadn't swung, but he didn't argue.

He was disappointed but consoled himself by thinking of his next turn. In the third inning he got up again, this time only wanting to meet the ball. He loosened his grip on the bat and concentrated, shutting out of his mind Willie, home runs, and everything else except the ball. "I took my stance," he recalled, "and looked the pitcher in the eye. The pitch was made and I swung with all the strength that was in me. The fans stood up and cheered as the ball sailed over the fence. I don't know what I thought of as I trotted around the bases, but as I came into home plate I began to see my teammates who had gathered there to greet me."

George lived, ate, and slept baseball. He began to keep a scrapbook of all Braves press clippings in the local paper, and occasionally the name George Foster would find its way into an article as the shortstop who knocked in the winning run, the job George liked best of all.

He also collected stories of famous ballplayers like Jackie Robinson, the first black player to be allowed into the majors; Roy Campanella, the great Dodger catcher; and of course, Willie Mays. These men, more than any he knew personally, were important to George, because as big leaguers they were respected black men in a mostly white world. His dream to follow in their footsteps influenced everything he did.

Because he only weighed 70 pounds, George couldn't depend on slugging home runs as others in the league like Dave Kingman could—he hit only four in his first season—so he worked hard instead on his fielding and speed. The effort paid off. He was

*As an alternate (second row, right) on the Little League All-Star team, 1961. Dave Kingman is second from left, front row.*

*As an El Camino Giant (front row, left) in 1962.*

chosen as an alternate for the Little League all-star game and the following year he made the regular all-star team as an El Camino Giant. "Wow!" he said to his mother. "I want to play for the San Francisco Giants, and I'm already a Giant."

He cared fiercely about each game, and his mother remembers, "If he didn't win he used to get real angry. I'd tell him Willie Mays doesn't win all the time. Sometimes you're up, sometimes you're down. You can't win 'em all. But he had his heart and mind on it from the beginning. When he lost you couldn't live with him. After a losing game I once gave him a ten-cent ticket to buy something to drink and he tore it in two. 'Why'd you do that?' I asked him. 'They could've won if they'd tried,' he said."

Although baseball was his first and deepest love, by the time George reached Leuzinger High School in Hawthorne he'd become a good enough athlete to play both varsity basketball and football as well. He learned quickly though, that weighing 128 pounds in baseball is very different from football. "I was fast," George recalls, "but when you're that light you have to be." Both his mother and his baseball coach wanted him off the football field and basketball court because of his size, and because if he were injured he could lose a playing season of baseball. The coach felt George should concentrate on one sport, baseball.

The coach's fears came true in George's senior year. During one basketball game late in the season he turned too quickly to duck a guard and felt his right knee buckle. He fell onto the knee and heard something crack. His shinbone had broken and he was out of action for his last year of high school baseball.

The break proved to be a "blessing in disguise," as George later called it. His mother had taught him that misfortunes could prove to be beneficial, and this one gave him a deferment from the army that allowed him to pursue without interruption his goal of playing in the major leagues.

Even though George graduated with scholastic

*George as a varsity basketball player in his senior year at Leuzinger High School, 1966.*

honors, his reason for going to nearby El Camino Junior College in the fall of 1967 was to play baseball and be drafted by a professional team right away. No longer small and frail, because he had lifted weights to build himself up to 185 pounds of solid muscle, George was ready for the baseball scouts' eyes. Any team would do, of course, but he secretly hoped it might be a Giant scout who wanted him. To be a Giant, to play beside Willie Mays, were dreams he'd carried since he was six years old. Now he was determined to make them come true.

## 2

# Say Hey, George

George was so eager to play baseball that he began playing on a Connie Mack team in the fall of 1967. At each game he hoped to see a scout, but he was always disappointed. George wasn't the sensation scouts traveled miles to see, and so he didn't attract the attention of any big league teams. Just as he was getting discouraged, he got a lucky break, one that would change his life. Scout Jack French described in a letter to a friend how he first met him.

> It was a nice sunny day at Torrance Park. A Connie Mack League game was scheduled between Hawthorne and the Red Devils. I got there just before the teams started taking infield practice. That's when I first laid my eyes on George Foster—throwing in from left field. I liked his throwing, so I made a notation in my little book about that. I was still probing the whole team for talent as the practice

continued. The shortstop had interested me when I saw Leuzinger High School during the season, and I particularly wanted to see their third baseman play. These are the two main reasons I was attracted to the game. As for the tall, skinny, black kid in left, he was just a body at the time doing his best to "fill out" the big number 3 on his back. I'd never seen him play before, and it looked like I'd never see him play again.

I guess it was during Foster's second time at bat that I realized I was looking at something outstanding. I liked his stance and the way he held his bat back. When he swung, I noticed the good power swing he had, but it was still raw and irregular. He didn't knock the cover off the ball that afternoon, although he did drop in a base hit. But it was his batting actions while swinging and missing, or fouling 'em off, that impressed me.

Although he has demonstrated since that he is a better than average runner, nothing happened that day to demand him to run at top speed. So I had to judge his running speed by the way he loped to his left field position, and his reactions on a couple of fly balls hit his way. My findings were that his running was at least adequate (and, in my heart, I was gambling that he could do better). With these calculations determined, George had "filled the bill" as a prospect. My next job was to interview him for the Giants by filling out his personal information on a card.

I noticed some of the Hawthorne players were beginning to straggle behind the stands, clear around to the first base side to get a drink of water between innings. George Foster was one of these. Meanwhile, I slipped down from my seat and waited to intercept him when he returned underneath the stands back of home plate. Several players passed by. Then along came George. He was alone.

"Hi, Foster! I'm Jack French, scout for the San Francisco Giants. You've made an impression on me today, and I'd like to get some information from you."

"Hi! Glad to meet you." He looked surprised.

Together, we filled out the card and I told him that I'd ntoify him to come out later in the fall to play on the Giant Rookies in the Scout League after the Connie Mack League ended. He told me that he didn't play baseball in his senior year at Leuzinger because of a basketball injury. The complete interview lasted about a minute and a half. He spoke with a soft high-pitched voice and with some hesitation. I thought I could detect an attitude of modesty and confidence in his shy answers to my questions.

At the end of our meeting, George looked over his shoulder, smiled politely, and said "Thanks a lot" as he walked away.

He was drafted by the Giants in January of 1968, signing his contract after playing at El Camino College that spring.

The rest of the story is baseball history.

A *Giant* rookie team. Move over, Willie Mays! "How lucky could a guy be," thought George. It was his dream come true, to be picked by the team he'd loved all his life.

After several games on the rookie team in California during the summer of 1968, nineteen-year-old George left for the Giants' Class A farm team in Medford, Oregon. As he boarded the bus for his long ride, he felt both elated that he would finally be playing professional baseball yet sad that he would be leaving home. He was sure he wanted to play, but he wasn't nearly as sure how he'd feel being away from his warm and supportive family.

At first, training camp was like being a new kid

*Heading for Medford, Oregon, 1968.*

at school again. Even though most of the guys were as green as he was, they seemed more assured and less nervous. They joked and talked easily with one another, occasionally boasting of their ability, but George was tongue-tied and rarely spoke to anyone. For many of the rookies, talking and telling jokes eased the pressure of competition and the loneliness of being away from home.

George had let off steam and shared his feelings with his family or with a good friend, but he had no friends in Medford, where he remained isolated from the others. Player-coach Leon Wagner remarked, "You're lucky if George says ten words a week." But when he assisted the team with his speed in the outfield, and when he drove in runs with his bat, no one cared how quiet the thin center fielder was.

George played hard every day, taking extra batting practice to become as good a hitter as he was a fielder. He already was a good defensive player, but now he wanted to be a fine all-around player. He also hoped he would improve enough to leap from A to AAA, and that would take work. "The Phoenix AAA manager said if I had a good year in A," George recalled, "he'd put me on his team." After that, every game became as important as the World Series to George, no matter how many games he played. Later in his career he would struggle for the motivation he had that first year in the minors.

The effort paid off when he moved to Fresno in 1969, where he showed himself ready for AAA baseball. With an impressive .321 average he became a California League all-star and a league leader with 85 runs batted in. RBI's were becoming George's specialty. He felt more driven to hit when there were men on base. "I feel needed then," he'd say.

Near the end of the season the San Francisco Giants were curious about the promising outfielder in Fresno, so they brought him up to play in the nine remaining games. It was George's first taste of the majors. The game he remembered best was against the Dodgers in Los Angeles. He'd been to Dodger Stadium a few times before as a fan, but it didn't prepare him for his first professional appearance there on a bright sunny Sunday.

He carefully suited up in the black and orange colors he'd dreamed about since he was six, adjusted his cap, and felt ten feet tall. Even if it was only temporary, he was proud to be a San Francisco Giant. Leaving the clubhouse, he trotted to the batting cage, feeling awkward among the Giant stars. Willie McCovey, Bobby Bonds, and Willie Mays were laughing with one another and didn't notice George staring at them. As he looked up into the stands, which were already quite full, he drew in his breath. If two hundred people showed up at a Fresno game, that was a lot. The Giants and Dodgers drew 30,000! "Better not look," he told himself. Scout Jack French remembered the game well:

"It was the top of the tenth inning of a one to one ball game. Claude Osteen had gone all the way for the Dodgers. It would have been over by now, but in the eighth inning Osteen had made the mistake of grooving one to Ron Hunt, who hit one of his rare homers.

"As Osteen completed his warm-up pitches, George Foster stepped up to the plate.

"After the announcement that Foster was now batting as the new left fielder, Osteen glanced down to get the sign from catcher Tom Haller. Finally, after negative nods, he backed off the mound and motioned for his catcher. Being a veteran of many campaigns, he wasn't about to have his bread and butter taken away by an untried rookie. So Haller trotted out near the mound and they had a meeting on how to pitch to George.

"Finally, sensing that he had some valuable information that might aid the two old pros, young Ted Sizemore bolted from his second base position to join the meeting. Being fresh out of the minors himself, he thought he remembered playing against George, as well as "the book" on how to pitch to him.

"The conference finally broke up when their heads snapped with affirmative nods, and they returned to their positions.

> "Osteen pitched and George connected solidly. It was a line drive that he pulled down the third base line. The ball struck the corner of the bag and ricocheted against the stands near the Dodger dugout. Maury Wills, backing up the play, finally retrieved the ball at the foul line (near the outfield cut of the infield) as Foster crossed the bag at first. Third baseman LeFebvre was dusting himself off after attempting to spear Foster's drive.
>
> "This was Foster's first major league base hit. It was the only plate appearance George made that day. The Dodgers won the game in the 11th 2–1."

After the season, *The Sporting News* took note of George: "Foster, a nineteen-year-old Hawthorne, California, youth who was with Fresno through the '69 campaign, may well be a regular Giant outfielder one day."

The following year George played in Phoenix, Arizona, his last year in the minors before being called up. His solid .308 average at the year's end convinced the Giant front office that after three minor league seasons he might be ready for the big leagues, so they called him up in the spring of 1971 to join the club for spring training in Tampa, Florida. Inspired by the opportunity, George was determined to make the final squad and travel north with the team in April. He played his heart out, taking extra practice in everything, but especially batting. He even

WIDE WORLD PHOTOS

*A San Francisco Giant, 1971.*

put ten pounds on his agile frame in the hope it would give him the power the Giants were known for. George was playing well but couldn't afford to let up for a moment—he'd come too far. Until he saw his name on the final list he refused to believe he was a Giant, and even afterwards it was hard to believe he'd reached his life-long goal.

George was still very shy, especially so around the star players. During spring training when he saw his name next to Bobby Bonds on the roommate schedule, he remembered, "I was sure it was a mistake. But Bobby chose me because he wanted to bring me out." Bobby Bonds recalled, "I guess it was almost two weeks before George even talked to me. He'd just go off in a corner, sit and not say a word. After two weeks, I got him to eat breakfast with me. He felt if he talked he'd be bothering you. Also, he was afraid to ask questions because he might seem dumb."

Bonds dragged George along to interviews, anywhere there were reporters or questions to help him get used to the public exposure. After awhile George didn't mind the questions too much but was sure he'd never want to speak in front of groups like the outgoing Bobby Bonds did. Even so, the brief time he spent with Bonds helped him not to be withdrawn and tight, especially after losing a game. He began to joke a little in the privacy of the clubhouse but still avoided the press and fans.

When the season began, George was the fourth outfielder behind Willie Mays in center field, Bonds in left field, and Ken Henderson in right field. He didn't get to play often, but when he did, he displayed his fine ability. He says about his first game as a full-fledged Giant: "My first game was against the Dodgers at Candlestick and I was very nervous, because I knew everyone at home would watch it on T.V. But I got my first hit off Don Sutton and I made a pretty good catch."

In the beginning he thought he could adjust to being a pinch hitter. His first encounter with St. Louis Cardinal pitcher Bob Gibson resulted in a homer over the left field fence that ruined Gibson's shutout and won the game for the Giants. A week later he hit another homer off Ferguson Jenkins that helped to defeat the Cubs.

But after his homers off these great pitchers, he returned once again to the bench. "I always knew when I filled in for a hurt fielder," George said "that no matter how well I did, they'd come back into the lineup." He was anxious to play, but the Giants didn't need him. After playing every day in the minors, George was restless and disappointed with only occasional appearances, but when he expressed his unhappiness someone was always quick to tell him how lucky he was just to be a Giant. His frustration at not playing interfered with his concentration, and he began to slump.

All his life he had wanted to be a Giant, but his dreams hadn't prepared him for sitting on the bench.

# 3
# Frustration

Memorial Day, 1971. On the bench as usual, George was clapping and whistling for the team, but he didn't feel right. The lineup was strange that night—they had an infielder, Jimmy Rosario, in the outfield. George wondered why they weren't playing him.

Fellow bench sitter Frank Johnson sat near George listening to the radio. "Hey, George," he said suddenly, "You've been traded." Used to the kidding that goes on among ballplayers, George ignored him and continued to concentrate on the game. Still, when Giant manager Charlie Fox walked by him after the game without saying anything, George breathed more easily. "Everything's okay, Johnson was just pulling my leg," he thought.

But then it happened. As he walked into the clubhouse he saw a crowd by his locker ready to congratulate him—he'd been traded to the Reds. His heart sank but he shook hands and tried to smile. Traded! The Giants were in first place and he wanted to play in the World Series. The Reds were at the bottom of the National League West.

He listened carefully to the details of the trade and discovered to his amazement that he'd been traded for Frank Duffy, a backup shortstop, and Vern Geishert, a pitcher, both of whom were in the minors. George had a .267 average with ten home runs. Reporters tried to get his feelings about the trade, but he was so crushed he could hardly speak. The Giants had been his team since he was a boy, and he couldn't imagine being anything else.

The trade, which was protested immediately by the other players, was one the Giants would soon regret. Vern Geishert never pitched for them and Frank Duffy was traded to the Cleveland Indians a year later.

The Reds were delighted to have George on their team, but he couldn't shake off the hurt and rejection he felt from the trade. He also missed his friends in the Giant organization, where after three years he was beginning to feel at home. His mind was so far from baseball that, at 22, he was ready to end his career. Lonely, confused, and in a slump, he went home to get his family's advice.

His mother was sorry about the trade, yet she was clear about his future. "Quit! After all these years you've put into baseball?" she asked him. "No, things are tough now, but you've got to stick with it." So George returned to Cincinnati and resolved to make the most of the situation.

The best thing about the trade was that he played every day because center fielder Bobby Tolan was injured. Being in the starting lineup also exposed him to pitchers that he had never faced on the Giants. Later that year he played against the Giants and hit a grand slam home run, the first of his career. He should have been thrilled, but instead he was somber. "I didn't get any special joy out of hitting that slam against the Giants," he said after the game. "I have too many friends on that team. I could just as easily still be with them."

Although in his first 19 games with the Reds he hit a powerful .354 and managed to play center field without error, he couldn't maintain the pace and his average plummeted. Reds manager Sparky Anderson took George off the regular roster, replacing him with Cesar Geronimo. The effect was devastating. By losing his spot in the lineup, the old frustration he felt as a Giant returned, and he began to doubt his ability.

At the season's end he had a .242 average with 13 homers and 58 RBI's. Because of this record he couldn't count on a regular place on the roster for the following season. He hoped his power and speed would win him the right field position, but in the spring of 1972

UPI

*George is congratulated by teammate Johnny Bench after hitting a grand-slam home run against the Giants, September 16, 1971.*

George found himself platooned in the outfield again, to be played only against left-handed pitchers. Because he knew that he couldn't be counted on when he was at bat, Sparky's decision was understandable, but sitting on the bench made him feel worse.

Still, there were moments that reminded George of his power. On June 1 the Reds, trailing the Los Angeles Dodgers in the National League West by 1½ games, brought in George to face the Astros' left-handed pitcher, Dave Roberts. The Astros were leading 3–2 in the third inning, but the Reds had the bases loaded when George came up to bat. George, who at the time was hitting .167, hit Roberts' first pitch into the bleachers. The Reds went on to win the game 12–4.

Despite the grand slam home run, George was still played sparingly for the rest of the season. He'd always dreamed of being on a pennant winning team, with him playing an important part of the victory. Instead he sat by the water cooler most of the time and watched the Reds win without him.

Worse than that, when the Reds finally did beat the Dodgers, George discovered that Sparky had no plans to play him in the pennant playoffs against the World Champion Pittsburgh Pirates. He wanted to do more than just sit and watch his team struggle through the playoff games. After the fourth game he stayed up a long time in his room, daydreaming about the final game. "One time I saw myself jumping on the plate with the winning run," he said.

The Pirates and Reds were playing the final game at Riverfront Stadium in Cincinnati and the tension crackled on both teams. The Pirates wanted to prove they were still the champions and the Reds wanted the chance to be in a World Series. The last time they had won the World Series was in 1940.

By the last game the teams were tired from the long season and the tough playoffs, but George was raring to go. In the ninth inning each were on their fourth pitcher, with Pittsburg holding onto a frail 3–2 lead. The Reds had been in this situation before, but no game that year had meant so much.

Pirate manager Bill Virdon brought in right hander Dave Giusti in the bottom of the ninth to finish the Reds. George had been hoping he'd be brought in, but when he saw the right hander he resigned himself to the bench.

Then Johnny Bench homered to right-center, tying the game, and the fans erupted from their nervous silence and the stadium was charged with excitement. Nearly everyone was standing now and would stay that way until the end. Tony Perez singled and represented the winning run. But Perez was a slow runner and the Reds needed speed.

Sparky looked down the bench and pointed to George to pinch-run for Perez. The winning run depended on George. He'd dreamed his bat would bring in the key run, but it turned out his long legs would have to do it. He jumped up and sprinted to first base to loosen the stiffness he felt from sitting on the bench. When Dennis Menke singled and moved George to second and in scoring position, Dave Giusti was off to the showers. Bob Moose was brought in to put out the fire. Cesar Geronimo hit a long fly that allowed George to tag up and move to third. He was ready to run on anything.

After Darrel Chaney hit a weak pop fly to second for the second out, pinch hitter Hal McRae stepped into the batter's box determined to be the hero of the game. Moose remembered that McRae was a good fastball hitter, so he sent him a slider that he fouled off. He whipped another to McRae that just missed the plate. Alex Grammas, third base coach, then leaned over to George and whispered, "Be ready in case one gets loose."

On the next pitch George saw it was going in too low. "By the time it hit the dirt I was moving and when it bounced high, I really took off," George said breathlessly, minutes after he ran home on Moose's wild pitch that won the game for the Reds 4–3. "Who would have ever thought the game would end like this?" he asked, laughing. It wasn't the way George had imagined it, but he was part of the playoff victory.

The pinch run put him into the public eye for the first time nationally, and people began to ask, "Who is this George Foster?" The press began to write about his early friendships with Willie Mays and Bobby Bonds, and the inevitable comparisons to these players followed. Even though George had once modeled his playing after Mays, he learned soon enough that "each guy has to be himself to reach his own potential." He no longer wanted to be the "new Willie

UPI

*George is greeted by his teammates after scoring the winning run in the final game of the 1972 playoffs. Pinch hitter Hal McRae is on left.*

or Bobby." The only things they all shared were, according to George, "that we were black and we were strong. There's only one Willie Mays and only one Bobby Bonds."

There was only one George Foster, too, but it would take time before he could know just how great he could be. The feeble .200 he had hit in his 59 games didn't make him feel quite as confident as he once felt. That winter George returned to Hawthorne and decided that rather than brood about the past year and worry about the future, he would study accounting. Baseball was his love, but it looked like he'd better know about something else.

Even so, when he got the news midway through spring training that he had been demoted to the minors, he was shocked. "My baseball career—if you could call it that—had hit bottom," George recalled.

He was caught in a terrible circle that kept him from playing his best. First the Giants had brought him up as a fourth outfielder. While he was feeling bad about not being played, he was hurt further by the trade. By the time the Reds played him regularly, his confidence had deserted him, and he slumped and lost his playing spot.

The newspapers confused and frightened George by making so much of his being sent down. They all had reasons for his slump and made predictions he would never be a Mays or Bonds. "I was listening to other people's assessments of my ability instead of believing in myself," he said. Once again he turned to his family for advice to help him make a decision about whether to play or to quit. After talking to them he decided to go to the Indianapolis farm club. "I knew if I stayed in Cincinnati I'd remain a part-time player," he reflected, "But by going down there I'd regain the qualities of determination, desire, concentration, and confidence that I'd lost sitting on the bench."

He wouldn't quit, at least not yet.

# 4

# Growing Up Down on the Farm

"My mother taught me that things would get better, to look on the bright side of things," George remembered. "And when things were tough she told me to stick with it." Those words often crossed his mind after he was sent to the Indianapolis AAA farm club. The fine, full ball parks, good hotels, and airplanes were just memories to George now. He didn't know if he'd ever see the big leagues again, and he was scared. His first minor league experience was exciting, but this one was painful. "I suddenly didn't have a goal anymore," he said. "There was no focus, no purpose to my life. I was confused and frightened."

His confusion affected his game. "He got off to a horrible start down there," according to Cincinnati Reds owner Bob Howsam. Howsam had been eager to have George on the team back in 1971, and like everyone else was mystified by his erratic hitting. He'd seen enough young ballplayers, however, to know that sitting on the bench can do terrible things to a player's confidence. "I began to believe all sorts of negative things about myself," George said of that time.

Howsam and Sparky Anderson agreed that George might do better with a year in the Reds' farm system. They certainly didn't want to trade him, because they felt he had so much potential. From his strong forearms to his powerful legs they saw the makings of a great slugger. But they also knew that the great player must have more than a body—he must have the right mental attitude as well. They hoped George would mature in Indianapolis. He'd been around for a while, but he was still only 24 years old.

As a professional ballplayer he would have to possess stronger inner resources to survive and stay on a major league team. He couldn't depend upon playing everyday, a hitting streak, or the crowd's roar to keep himself going. He needed something else to give him the courage to persist when times were hard.

One important change in his life came from his friendship with Indianapolis outfielders Ken Griffey and Ed Armbrister. For the first time since he left home he felt close enough to share his feelings with other people. Ken, who roomed with George in Indianapolis and continued to be his roommate as a Red, said about that time: "At first we had a hard time communicating because he was so upset about being

*At Bush Stadium with the Indianapolis farm club. Ken Griffey is in foreground.*

sent down, but after a while we'd have such a good time on the field just laughing that he forgot his situation and started to play ball."

His new friends helped George to relax and enjoy baseball again. "I began to hit the ball better, harder. My total performance became more aggressive and confident," he said. But the most important addition to his life was the Bible. He had been brought up with religion at home, but he'd forgotten about it after he had left. By studying the Bible, he gained perspective and direction again.

Hits began to bounce off his bat consistently, but not until he found an unusual looking black bat with a whip-thin handle. George described the discovery of his bat like this: "In the minors, I always used everyone else's bat. I kept switching and never found a model I could stick with. For a time I used a Jackie Robinson bat with a thick handle when I was going for base hits, but I couldn't get distance. This guy named Hal King had a bat that was hickory stained. I asked him if I could use it. It felt comfortable and gave me good distance. With a 33 ounce bat I'd hit the ball with all my might and it would go to the warning track. With the 35 ounce black bat I didn't have to swing as hard and it would go further. When I got back to the big leagues I wanted to be sure I got that same one. I thought it only came in black, so I ordered a hickory stained 35 ounce, 35 inch bat."

He was earning praise for his glove, too. Vern Rapp, manager of the Indianapolis Indians and later manager of the St. Louis Cardinals, said about the outfield of Foster, Griffey and Armbrister: "These can be the finest three players I've ever managed as far as outfield talent is concerned. They all have excellent speed, good range and fine arms. This could be the finest outfield in the minor leagues. Foster has fine qualities of leadership. He can take charge of the outfield and he has a good attitude. He's a very aggressive player."

Once he developed consistent hitting power, George no longer wondered whether he would stay in baseball. He had found his way back. In the past he'd always hit an occasional long ball, but his concentration was "random," as he described it. "It was at Indianapolis that I learned how to have all the facets of a game together before it starts. That way I'm really ready," George said.

By September 1 George was relaxed and at peace with himself, yet far more aggressive at the plate. He was hot with his bat, not with his anger. It was a good thing, too, because the Reds needed him in Cincinnati for their drive to win the division title, so Sparky Anderson recalled George from Indianapolis.

In his first game back he was brought in to pinch-hit in a game against Atlanta. He homered in the eighth inning, driving in three runs and tying the game at 3–3. Anderson, watching the distance of the home run, shook his head and said, "When George gets into a pitch, no one hits a ball harder than he does—not Willie Stargell, Willy McCovey, or Lee May." George overheard the comparison, but being compared didn't bother him anymore. All that mattered was whether he could help bolster a tired team in the stretch of a tight race. In the ninth inning he drove in two more runs and the Reds won 5–3. George had driven in every Red run on the scoreboard.

He played in seventeen more games, giving his teammates a preview of the new George. He delivered four homers, drove in nine runs in 39 at bats, and helped to keep the Reds in the race. "Not until after George joined us," Anderson told reporters, "did we realize he had improved so much in his hitting since last year."

One of George's biggest fans was a competitor. His old roommate and friend, Bobby Bonds, had followed George's ups and downs since they first met, and now he saw a turning point in George's career. "I'm happy for George any time he does well, but at the same time I never want to see him beat us," Bonds exclaimed after losing a game to the Reds in which George had belted two homers off Ron Bryant. "George has a lot of ability," Bobby said wistfully. "That's why I still say I wish the Giants had never traded him away."

Besides helping to win games, George also lifted his team's spirits by easing the pressure on the few healthy players who felt they had to hold up the entire team. His timely hits gave them hope that despite the team injuries the Reds again could win the division race, and they were right. The Reds clinched their division and faced the Mets in the pennant playoffs.

George should have been ecstatic, but he wasn't. He was ineligible to participate in postseason games because he'd joined the team too late in the season. Still, Bob Howsam wanted George present to offer moral support to the team he'd helped into the playoffs, so he invited him to stay for the games. After the first two, however, George wished he had refused the invitation. The day before he watched as Mets' left-hander Jon Matlack blanked the Reds 5–0. He had sat helplessly as Sparky called up three pinch hitters. "And each time Sparky started to call out a name I knew it wasn't going to be mine," said George.

George sat in full uniform, head down, speaking so softly reporters strained to hear how he was feeling during the playoffs. When asked how it felt not to be eligible, he was careful with his answer, to be sure they understood what he thought was obvious—anytime you have to sit on the bench when you know you can do the job, you feel terrible.

After Matlack's game and the reporters' questions, he left New York. "This is plain torture," he said by way of explanation, as he packed his bag to return home. "I'll be watching the games on television and pulling for the guys as hard as I can, but I just can't sit in the dugout any longer knowing there's no way I'm going to get into a game."

Sparky Anderson understood George's feelings. "George is an extremely sensitive young man. In the same position I might feel as he does," he said.

George returned home and found himself just as frustrated but at least it was in the privacy of his mother's living room. Nobody there asked him how he felt when he watched the Mets' Tom Seaver take the final victory from the Reds 7–2. The Reds lost their bid to the pennant while George watched helplessly.

"All right," he thought to himself, as he switched off the T.V. "Wait until next year." He was ready for the smoke.

# 5

# The Black Bat Returns

Dressed once again in the crisp white and red Cincinnati uniform that bore his new number 15, George looked around the spring training camp and spotted familiar faces. Ken Griffey and first baseman Dan Driessen were talking in the dugout, Pete Rose, in a deep crouch, was taking batting practice, and shortstop Davey Concepcion was sitting in the outfield doing stretch exercises. It was great to be back. He couldn't wait to play for the Reds again, but more importantly his return represented the positive change in his character.

Every spring he had worried about too many things—the reporters, the starting lineup, his performance, all of which kept his head spinning. But in 1974 his worries were past him after his good year in Indianapolis both as an athlete and as a man. Sparky Anderson noticed George seemed looser and less shy upon his return. He watched with satisfaction as George mingled and talked with his friends. "He'll never be a loudmouth," Sparky said, "but his new attitude will make him a better ballplayer."

It was time for batting practice. Pitching coach Larry Shepard stepped behind the protective net at the mound and batting coach Ted Kluszewski positioned himself near the batting cage. Since training had just begun Shepard would go easy on his pitches, but Sparky and Klu would watch the batters closely to catch any problems.

Kluszewski a once-great Cincinnati slugger himself, looked at George's build with admiration. George was built like his bat, broad at the top and narrow at the bottom, with a 42″ chest and a 30″ waist. He worked hard to stay in shape with calisthenics, watching his weight, and eating only healthy foods. He didn't drink liquor or coffee, or smoke—his only indulgence being an occasional vanilla milk shake. His effort and discipline had contributed to the makings of a great player.

George stepped into the batting cage following Davey Concepcion. At the first pitch he swung with all his might and hit the ball to the warning track. Several players nodded approval; but Klu frowned—something was wrong with his swing. He watched carefully, noting George's stance, stride, and swing as he took his next pitches, most of which he hit well.

Suddenly Klu shouted to Shepard, "Pitch him inside." George swung awkwardly and missed the pitch.

As Klu suspected, George's split-second lateness stemmed from his having two swings, one for inside and one for outside pitches. He would have to develop one swing, because if he guessed the wrong swing he'd miss the ball. "We had to change his thinking about inside pitches," Klu said. "He didn't like them because they can hurt your hands and because you look funny jumping out of the way."

George didn't like to look funny; he liked to look good. His speed and good eye in the outfield made his catches look easy rather than thrilling. And when it came to sliding, he only slid when it was absolutely necessary. "I always get hurt when I slide," he'd say, adding slyly, "I'd rather hit it out of the park and trot around the bases."

Inside pitches were a problem, and Klu taught him to reach those balls sooner, and to use the same powerful level swing on every pitch. To get to the ball sooner, he had to be quick enough to bring his bat around like a whip.

Besides the speed of his bat, George had great strength. Klu would say, "Foster can call on a dual source of power. Guys like me hit home runs with brute strength. Others, like Henry Aaron, did it with quick hands. George has both." Actually, George surprised himself after the lessons with Klu. "I was amazed at the power I had," he said.

Both Sparky and Klu worked on George's confidence, too. "The big secret to his success is that now *he* knows he's a great hitter," Klu said. "He believes now. We knew he was a great hitter and could do it, but it took time to get him to believe it, too." The best part about Klu's tips were that George found he could hit the ball more consistently. "He's becoming a disciplined hitter," Sparky said approvingly.

George had been playing baseball nearly all his life and had had many coaches. Yet there was still much to learn about the art of hitting, and now he saw there was no limit to what he could do. He used to say that although he couldn't hit 30 or 40 homeruns, he could hit 15 or 20. But now he saw there was no point in thinking that way. "Why put limits on what you can do?" he said.

Sparky was again managing an extraordinary team with such players as Rose, Bench, Morgan, Perez, Geronimo, and Concepcion. George knew he would be platooned again, but this year he'd made his peace, and the anger which had interfered before was gone. "I still wasn't in the starting lineup, but my playing was improving steadily," he recalled. "I no longer let what other people said bother me. I was determined to get out on the field and do the best job I could."

Sooner or later, if he was meant to play regularly,

he would. In the meantime, sitting on the bench still wasn't fun, but George put himself mentally into each game. He was ready to pinch-hit, pinch-run, play against lefties, or anything Sparky wanted. His job was to be patient, to believe in himself, and to be ready when called. He practiced every day and gave special attention to keeping his forearms strong; like Ted Williams a generation before, at any spare moment, even in the on-deck circle right before he hit, he squeezed a small rubber ball in his hand. Besides being physically strong, now he was inwardly strong enough to stay calm when he wasn't playing. This strength would also keep him calm a few years later when the world would be staring pop-eyed at his awesome statistics.

After the season he went back to California and played baseball with the neighborhood children. He'd round up six or seven kids ranging from six to nine and go to the park. With the youngest he would begin by rolling the ball until they became confident of their catches. Then he'd bounce it, throw it underhand, and finally overhand. Both George and the youngsters would be delighted with their accomplishment.

Sometimes he'd put a little game together with all the kids against him while he batted lefty. "They'd enjoy it because I took the time to play and I'd enjoy seeing them like baseball," he said. Because no one played ball with him when he was small, he took

*With his mother, Regina Foster, at her home in Hawthorne, California, January, 1974.*

special pleasure in these games. If George saw one of them swinging up, he tried to get him to swing evenly, but the main point for the young children was to have fun.

If the older girls and boys wanted more tips, he told them to hit in front of the plate and to hit with authority. "It's important to have strong hands and wrists, and be sure to use a bat that's comfortable," he said. "A big bat that you can't whip around won't work. Also, use whatever stance you find comfortable that day or what you think the pitcher dictates."

He also reminded them not to grip the bat too tightly, just to squeeze it enough so the ball wouldn't knock it out of their hands. Even though George no longer needed to choke the bat, he suggested it for better bat control, especially when the batter had two strikes. Most of all he told them to practice, practice, and to be patient.

"I want to help kids to believe in themselves," George said, "no matter if it's through sports or something else. You have to believe you can do the job, know you have to work and practice to do it, and not give up if you have a bad outing. Sports can give you the confidence to do anything that is divinely yours."

# 6

# Make Room

"Getting traded to Cincinnati was a blessing in disguise," George once said, "but it took maybe two years to realize it. All my struggles and difficulties to get me where I am now helped me to mature." Being black in a white world, being benched when he felt ready to play, being traded away from his only friends no longer hurt—the soul-searching and growing had been worth it. He wasn't a star or even a starting player, but he was a happy man in the spring of 1975. Still, it had been six years since he signed his first professional contract and he had yet to play as a regular in the majors. This had to be the year he made the starting lineup.

His big opportunity came in the opening game of the season. The score was tied at the end of the ninth, and with two outs and a man on third, it looked as if the game might go into extra innings. If they could only bring in the man on third, the Reds would win the game.

Reluctantly, Sparky Anderson gave George the chance. "Foster's a slow starter," he was quoted later. "I stuck him in out of desperation. There were no other right handers left."

George remembered that moment well, "My career was riding on what I could do at bat," he said. He was terribly nervous, but he controlled his feelings by telling himself he could do it. "You've got to think you can; otherwise you won't," he said to himself.

He swiveled his hips a little at the plate to loosen up and then let a couple of balls go by to see what the pitcher had that day. He hit the next pitch and began to run. "I had been warming the bench for nine innings and my legs were cramped," he recalled. "I couldn't seem to get myself moving. First base seemed a long, long way off, and I felt like I was running in slow motion. I tagged the base at about the same time the ball arrived. It was a split-decision, but the umpire called me safe, and we won the game."

From that game on, George played more and more. His teammates saw that he was a player they could count on, a player who could help them beat the Dodgers in the Western Division by driving in runs with his powerful bat. Pete Rose, the first player who spoke to George when he had joined the team in 1971 and who gave him his clubhouse name,

*Some of those black bats.*

"Yahtzee," helped him get a regular spot on the team.

The Reds had begun to slump in May and George was hitting .275 when Sparky Anderson asked Pete Rose to move to third base to make room for George in left field. "I could have told Sparky no, I won't do it," Rose said later. The outfield, after all, was named the Rose Garden, but Pete moved, because as he said, “I saw George was good and I felt he would help the team.” Pete was right and a year later the outfield was called Fosterville.

As soon as George joined the lineup, the slumping Reds began to turn around and George raised his average to .300, the highest he’d ever hit in the majors. His black bat became conspicuous for its effect as well as its color. At first the players kidded him about the bat and reporters asked him seriously if the color had importance. They played perfect straight men to George’s clowning. “I’m integrating the bat rack,” he’d tell the white reporters, and to brush off questions about his bat, he’d end the discussion by stating flatly, “It’s the man, not the bat, that counts.”

The reporters, who remembered George as introverted and shy when he first came to Cincinnati, were surprised at his quick, flippant replies. Many were happy that he was finally playing, because beside his ability, they had known enough players to value his exceptional decency. Hal McCoy, writer for the *Dayton Daily News,* said about him: “He’s my best friend on the team and he’s the greatest person in baseball. I mean as a person, not just a player. He never raises his voice, no matter how harassed he may be by fans. I asked him once if he’d let me use his name for Building Bridges, an organization for underprivileged kids. He said, ‘No, you’ll have more than my name. I'll be there, too.' "

Perhaps one of the best things about having to wait a long time for something you want very much is that when you get it, it's extra special. Every day when George came out of the clubhouse for practice, he'd check the lineup. Pasted in the dugout, usually scribbled hastily in pencil, he'd see "Foster" and feel great. The pleasure of seeing his name there, even if it were seventh or eighth, was wonderful. He dreamed of being number three or four someday, but for now he was glad just to be in the lineup.

If concentration had once eluded him, he had no trouble with it now. For the first time in his major league career, hits were consistently jumping off his bat. In August he batted safely in sixteen games, and during another stretch, he hit safely in 32 of 40 games. The chance to play regularly and to be in a tight pennant race was exhilarating, and George's bat spoke his feelings that summer.

"When men are on base or in scoring position, I feel more of a challenge. It's my job to bring in those runs," he said. He also had a better chance with men on base, because the pitcher, with more on his mind, was apt to make a mistake. He tried to sense the pitcher's thoughts as soon as he stepped into the batter's box. "Men on base," he'd think. "He doesn't want to walk me with our powerful lineup and he's afraid to give me anything good. Probably try a breaking ball." Frequently, George guessed right and won the contest.

This thinking required a readiness that George had to feel before he could step up to the plate. "There are different periods of time when I'm ready," George explained. "Maybe I get ready the night before the game or just before I get to the game. Sometimes it's not before I get into the batter's box."

*In this double exposure, Denny Doyle of the Boston Red Sox can't make the tag in time as George steals second base in the 1975 World Series.*

CINCINNATI ENQUIRER (FRED STRAUB) PHOTO

Some pitchers suspected that when George took a minute or two before he stepped up to the plate, he was trying to throw off their rhythm, but that wasn't true. "I'm just getting my concentration ready," he said. "If you go up there as if it's just another turn to hit, you'll be just another out. So the thing is taking time to get ready even if it's going to stall the game. The main thing is to be ready."

George's readiness helped the Reds make it to the World Series. By the end of the year he had kept his .300 average, with 23 homeruns and 78 RBI's, but the statistics only told part of the story. Sparky Anderson declared, "Having George in left field made the difference in our ball club winning the World Series."

# 7

# The Gentle Destroyer

The hazy Florida sun glared into George's eyes as he ran sideways to snare what seemed like the 500th ball that morning. He found it in the sun, whipped it into the infield and waited for the next fungo. After the long winter, spring training was exhausting but welcome.

On the next popup he squinted into the sky and nearly tripped over a briefcase in left-center field. It belonged to a photographer intent on catching George in action. Ken Griffey chuckled as George exclaimed, "This is ridiculous!" Through the fence he heard fans calling, "Hey, George, can you sign this?" Ball and pens, suspended by string, hung over the fence in the hope George would walk by and sign one.

"Everybody sure loves a winner," George thought wryly. Still, the attention from the press and fans was flattering. His contribution the year before had put him into the limelight with the other Red stars. It had been a long climb from his minor league days in Medford, Oregon, but every second had been worth it.

When he finished fielding he sprinted into the dugout before taking batting practice. He sat down, wiped the stinging sweat from his eyes, and began to concentrate on hitting. When George sat like that, unsmiling and quiet, friends Ken Griffey and Dan Driessen knew better than to talk to him.

Finally he stood, picked up his elegant bat, and walked to the batting cage. Every muscle poised and ready for the pitch, he caught the first one and rifled it to right field for what would have been a base hit. At the next pitch he swung gracefully but with enough power to arc it into the left field bleachers. The crowd responded and George permitted himself a smile. "That's it, that's the groove," he whispered as he stepped out of the cage. The extra practice had helped him to hit to all fields. It would keep pitchers on their toes and force the outfield to play him straight, because unlike Dave Kingman or Richie Hebner, George had become a spray hitter, a slugger who could hit the ball anywhere.

From the first day of spring training, 1976, George impressed everyone with his home runs. The sports writers in Tampa, who had always plenty of talented players to report about, momentarily forgot the others and concentrated on George Foster. Earl Lawson of *The Sporting News* wrote:

> Meanwhile, the talk in Florida was on George Foster, who has been quoted as saying his goal is to learn his full potential as a major league player. And this spring Red manager Sparky Anderson is hoping that Foster offered a hint as to what it might be when he rapped Grapefruit League pitching at a .444 clip to lead the Red regulars in hitting and topped the club with three homers and 16 rbi's. It's difficult to estimate just how much potential he has. There isn't a finer physical specimen on the Reds' Club.

The season began with the Reds as World Champions and they played like champions, mauling teams with scores such as these: Reds 10–Giants 2, Reds 13–Astros 2, Reds 11–Cards 2. As part of the Big Red Machine George played a vital part in those early victories as his average rose to .367, with 10 RBI's in the first five games.

Besides his bat, his arm, and speed in the outfield, George along with Geronimo and Griffey, made the Reds' defense the best in baseball. No baserunner took an extra base from them, and George enjoyed this respect. When the ball dropped in for a single, sometimes he got playful and didn't throw the ball to second right away. He'd stand holding it, wrist cocked, daring the runner to try for another base—but George's reputation for quick assists kept them at first.

The excitement in May, however, was George's bat. The best hitter in the league, he was picked as National League Player of the Month. In 26 games he had hit seven homers, driven in 31 runs, and had a fast .360 average to show for it. Red outfielder Bob Bailey exclaimed, "He's got a chance for a homer with every swing, he's so strong." Besides that, George was one of a handful of hitters who hit home runs yet maintained a high average. Average is often sacrificed for homers, and a .350 hitter usually doesn't hit many long balls.

Opposing pitchers, who the year before only knew George by his number, now knew his black bat only too well. Then they had faced him batting eighth in the lineup, often with no one on base, but this year in the sixth, fifth, or fourth spot, he was driving in runs and ripping open games. Sparky named him "The Destroyer," because he destroyed no-hitters, shutouts, and earned run averages with his long swing that reached many pitches.

A few games after he was chosen Player of the Month, his first recognition in major league baseball, he reached another first. He became a member of the exclusive "Red Seat Club" when he unleashed his twelfth home run into the top tier of the red seats at

Riverfront Stadium. Since the stadium opened in 1970, only six balls had ever landed there. The Reds were playing the Chicago Cubs when George came up to the plate with two outs in the sixth, and swung hard at Joe Coleman's pitch. The second it left his bat George knew it was gone, but I "thought the ball might go foul and I was leaning with it," he said after the game.

"What kind of pitch was it?" a reporter asked George.

"I don't know," he answered, "but after it got up there it was a lopsided Spalding."

Overhearing George's interview, Sparky added, "Anyone who hit a ball that far has to feel awful proud."

Someone asked Davey Concepcion, who rarely hit more than ten home runs a season, when he would put one into the red seats. "When I get to weigh 220 pounds," the slender shortstop said.

George wisecracked, "Concepcion will put a ball in the red seats when an usher leads him up there."

Ken Griffey, George's roommate, said wistfully, "George hits a ball into the red seats and I'm wishing I could get one as far as the green seats."

George was growing uneasy with all this talk about distance. "What difference does it make how far you hit the ball?" he said. "No matter what, you only get one trip around the bases."

Although a pitcher might grease, cut, or spit on a ball to make his pitch harder to hit, the batter is stuck with his bat. He must rely only on power, quick hands and a good eye to get his hit. Nevertheless, after seeing George hit his thirteenth and fourteenth homers the night before, Philly pitcher Jim Lonborg said, "The way Foster's hitting I'm going to have to check his bat before tomorrow's game." He was kidding, but some batters may have also believed George's bat was magic, because more and more sluggers, from Reggie Jackson to Dave Parker, were beginning to use black bats. "I should have taken a patent on that bat," George laughed.

George stood stiffly at attention, waiting to hear the All-Star game announcer at Veteran's Stadium in Philadelphia bark, "Cincinnati Reds' left fielder, George Foster!" He stepped forward, tipped his hat to the crowd and ignored the inevitable boos that Philly fans offered opposing teams. On the outside George looked calm, almost nonchalant about the game, but inside his heart was pounding with excitement. Along with teammates Johnny Bench, Pete Rose, Joe Morgan, Tony Perez, and Dave Concepcion, George represented the best in the National League. Besides that, his league-leading 72 RBI's persuaded both fans and players that he should be a starting player. He couldn't wait for the introductory ceremonies to be over so he could play ball with this special team.

The boos that greeted George quickly changed to cheers in the third inning when he drove in three runs with a 400 foot home run off Yankee ace Catfish Hunter. That homer, plus a key groundout that allowed Dodger Steve Garvey to score and help the National League to win 7–1, earned George the All-Star Most Valuable Player title. Thrilled to receive the gleaming trophy from ex-Giant star Monte Irvin, for a while he wasn't sure if Irvin was going to hand it over. "He was nervous and I was nervous," George recalled. "It was my first time to get the award and Irvin's first time to give it, so I didn't know when to take it and he didn't know when to give it." Finally, though, he did receive the trophy, which now holds a special place among other awards and baseball mementoes in his old room at his mother's home.

Now that George had earned two mid-season awards, talk of his earning the big MVP of the year began. Reds' second baseman, Joe Morgan, who had won the year before, felt George should get it, because "every time we win it's Foster and a different guy," Morgan said after a winning game. "Like tonight, Foster and Bench. In other games it's Foster and a pitcher—or Foster and another hitter."

It seemed as though nothing could stop him. As he continued hitting those long, long homers that brought base runners home to win games, he was picked Player

UPI

*Hitting a three-run homer in the third inning of the 1976 All-Star game to give the National League an early lead.*

UPI

*Receiving the All-Star Most Valuable Player Award from Monte Irvin.*

of the Month again for July. Sparky Anderson predicted that George would drive in 120 runs. After every game the reporters crowded around George's locker wanting interviews, and George was glad to oblige them. He'd had trouble in the past talking to the papers, even getting recognition he felt he deserved, but now he was getting plenty of attention—maybe more than he needed.

The reporters' constant talk of the MVP and the excitement of having already won three awards drove George to prove to the public that he could do it, that he could win the biggest award of all. He was certainly within reach—his average was in the .330's, his RBI's were tops, and the Reds were once again pennant contenders. But he felt he needed to win the Triple Crown, an almost impossible title that required being highest in average, homers and RBI's, if he were to be chosen MVP. He needed more home runs.

The pressure began to affect his game as he took more and more time in the batter's box in an effort to get his concentration on hitting the long ball. In the last 40 games of the season, though, no matter how hard he tried, he struck out often. His average fell daily. Except for the fatigue that plagues most players by August, he was fine physically, but something was wrong. He was concentrating all right, but on the wrong thing—the award.

UPI

*Being congratulated by coach George Scherger as he rounds third base after hitting a home run to put the Reds ahead in the first game of the 1976 playoffs.*

While George was struggling to get back into a hitting groove, the Reds remained in front and went on to win the playoffs over the Phillies in three straight games. And although Joe Morgan had replaced George as the big hitter in September, George still hit well to help the Reds beat the Yankees in a four game World Series sweep.

By the end of the season George's average had dropped to .306, a good average, but he was bitterly disappointed after his fabulous start. With 121 RBI's he won the RBI title, but he ended with only 29 home runs. He also won the Sporting News National League Player of the Year Award, but it wasn't enough. When he heard that Joe Morgan had won the MVP for the second year in a row, he couldn't hide his anger. "I should have won," he snapped. Immediately he regretted his words and apologized to Morgan, saying, "You have to practice what you preach, and I didn't."

After the World Series George went home, this time to his apartment in Cincinnati, to think about the past year and to learn from it. It had been a fantastic year beyond any expectation or dream, and it had reminded him again not to put limits on his ability. But the year had also challenged him as a person. He'd found himself so anxious for outside recognition that he'd become "too materially minded," as he put it. It had even caused him to envy his good friend, Joe Morgan.

UPI

*Making a catch against the wall during the 1976 playoffs.*

After each season, George always hoped the next year he would do better, but in 1976 he also hoped he'd learned his lesson. If there was one thing George Foster wanted to be more than a great ballplayer, it was to be a good person.

# 8
# A Late Blossom

The crowd roared its welcome as George stepped out of the Riverfront Stadium dugout to wait in the on-deck circle. He didn't look up at the fans, but their cheers excited him. Sometimes he tried to block out stadium noises, but tonight they motivated him as much as the butterflies in his stomach prepared him for the batter's box. He felt strong and fast that muggy July 14 evening in Cincinnati.

From a kneeling position he carefully watched Atlanta pitcher Dick Ruthven challenge Joe Morgan with fastballs. "Good," George thought to himself. "Let him try me, too."

Morgan struck out and George went to the plate, his mind focused on "seeing the ball and hitting it with authority." He no longer tried to hit the ball with everything in him—he knew that his natural swing could easily bring in a home run. Looking down he scratched the ground near the batter's box with his spikes very deliberately, making the box his turf and making the time his own.

Ruthven grew impatient. He wanted to get it over with. Pitching to George Foster was never fun, and furthermore he'd seen what George had done to a ball during batting practice that night—it had seemed like a full minute before it landed. Finally George stepped up to the plate and waited for the pitch. As he moved his wrists slightly the fat part of the bat made menacing little circles. Ruthven wound up and tried to get past George with an outside curve. Ball

*The famous swing, 1977.*

one. The next pitch was a strike, just breaking inside, and Ruthven began to think he might get past Foster. Then George thought, "It's going to be outside," and swung at the third pitch. At the crack of the bat the crowd cheered as he began his 26th home run trot.

The 1977 season was only half over. No question, he had "that feeling" and he was finding his pitch in nearly every game. The month before he'd been named June Player of the Month, because he had driven in thirty-eight runs.

In the third inning, George had that feeling again, and Ruthven couldn't escape. Anything he threw over the plate was in jeopardy. Sure enough, on the first pitch George belted the ball into the seats again for his second home run of the night. That was enough for Ruthven. But George wasn't through. The reliever also couldn't get away from "Black Beauty," George's name for his bat. At his last at bat, George, with his graceful classic swing, almost effortlessly sent the first pitch soaring into the stands for his third home run of the game.

The Reds won the game 7–1, and the winning pitcher was Tom Seaver. Especially glad it was Seaver, who had just been traded from the low-scoring Mets, George said, "I want to make good defensive plays and score some runs for him so he won't feel he's got to pitch a shutout to win a game." He kept his word three times that night. Seaver, who had lost many games for the Mets when he'd given up only one or two runs, shouted, "That Foster! He's fantastic!"

The next night the Reds faced Houston, and George was tempted to make it four homers in a row. "Maybe that's a record," he thought to himself as he faced the Houston pitcher. Instead he watched a pop fly drop into the centerfielder's glove and was sternly reminded of what had happened the year before when he'd chased numbers. He relaxed and next time

*With the three home-run balls he hit in one game on July 14, 1977, at Riverfront Stadium.*

up hit his 29th home run. "You never know how much you can do," he said happily after the game.

George hit twelve home runs in the month of July to bring his total to 32, the most he'd hit in any entire season. Writers suggested it would be his best year, but August was coming up, the hardest month in the majors, especially for a team that is not a contender. The Dodgers had grabbed first place in April and wouldn't let go, and the Reds were trailing them by twelve games. August was also the month of George's tailspin the year before. He was determined not to fall into the same trap of worrying about awards and records. "If it happens it happens," he calmly told excited reporters when they brought up the MVP award. He was even relaxed enough to tease the press. After a game Joe Morgan helped win, a crowd of reporters circled Morgan's locker instead of George's. One reporter looked over his shoulder and instead of seeing a colleague, saw George, pen and pencil poised, humorously imitating a reporter by asking questions with obvious answers. The reporter's surprised face elicited a mischievous grin from the usually serious George. It had taken a long time, but he could finally stay loose under great pressure.

George may have been calm, but every member of the Reds, many of them superstars themselves, were amazed by him. Joe Morgan kidded, "I've never seen anything like this, but a man with George's good habits deserves to hit fifty home runs." Johnny Bench confessed, "He makes me feel inadequate." Pete Rose summed up the feelings of all who watched George in the late summer of 1977, "He was a late blossom and now he's bleeping awesome."

On the first day of August George hit two home runs off Cub pitcher Steve Renko, thus assuring himself that the month would begin well. He than proceeded to hit a home run in each of the next two games. By the end of the month he had hit 11 for a total of 43, and to no one's surprise captured the August Player of the Month award. The award had special meaning for him because it was a mark of the consistency that had escaped him the year before.

Without the tension of a championship George had to keep his concentration in order to continue his phenomenal performance—his race with the calendar. Fifty was the number that popped up everywhere. One reporter asked him after his 43rd homer if he thought he'd reach 50. "Well, I'm 28 now," he said. "If I keep my health, live a clean life, and take vitamins, I think I'll reach 50." Sports fans and writers dug into record books and discovered that only three National Leaguers had surpassed 50 home runs in a season—Hack Wilson's 56 in 1930, Ralph Kiner's 54 in 1949, and Willie Mays' 52 in 1965.

"I saw the ball so well," George said about that time, "it seemed almost any pitch would do." One night he hit a pitch that came between his knees and ankles and drove it 375 feet. Anywhere his bat could reach was his pitch, and pitchers shuddered when they faced him. He was hitting a homer on the average of one in every twelve at bats, whether the pitcher was right or lefthanded.

If he were hitting for average, like Rod Carew, or to extend a hitting streak, like Pete Rose, the pitchers wouldn't have minded so much, but they hated to give up home runs. The pitchers vainly tried to get past him, rarely challenging him with a fastball. If the count were 3–1, they'd rather risk a pitch out of the strike zone. They made it harder for George to get something to hit, but he thrived on the contest. Mentally, it was as though he were playing the game of 1–2–3–shoot with one player trying to outwit the other in the number of fingers shown, and George was winning the contest most of the time. That, and being able to see the ball as though it were a grapefruit, accounted for his success.

By the end of the season, with a .320 average, he had racked up 52 home runs and 149 RBI's. He came within one RBI of being the second player to hit fifty home runs and drive in 150 runs in a season. Only Hack Wilson had done it. Besides catapulting him among baseball's immortals—he became the tenth man to hit 50 or more home runs in a season and all of the other nine were in the Hall of Fame—he also

WIDE WORLD PHOTOS

*George drives in his 149th run, October 2, 1977.*

destroyed several club records as well. His fifty-two homers erased Ted Kluszewski's mark of 49, and his RBI's wiped out Johnny Bench's 148. His 388 total bases replaced Frank Robinson's mark of 380 and were the most by any major league player since Henry Aaron amassed 400 in 1959. He also led the National League in home runs, runs batted in, total bases, and runs scored (124). Yet it was possible for him not to be chosen the Most Valuable Player of the Year.

The Most Valuable Player is usually the man most responsible for his team being a winner. Despite George's amazing record, the Reds finished eleven games behind the Dodgers. In forty-six years of the awards, only fifteen players had been named from a non-pennant winner.

Philly slugger Greg Luzinski, with 36 homers and 134 RBI's, was in a good position to be picked, because the Phillies were in first place in their division. Another advantage Luzinski possessed was his outgoingness and generosity. The year before, he bought a block of season tickets in the bleachers for poor children, and it had been widely publicized.

The people in Hawthorne knew that George always brought home shirts, balls, and bats for the kids, and they knew about the hours he spent talking to them individually and in groups, but he had done it without publicity. "You can't change yourself to get votes for the MVP," he told his friends. "If something is meant for you, then you'll get it." When he became a big leaguer, he saw players chat with strangers, sign dozens of autographs before a game and endorse products. At first he tried to imitate these players, but found it took too much energy. He'd just have to be himself and hope, as he said, "that the silence of George Foster would be heard."

## 9

# Most Valuable Person

"I was warned ahead I was a candidate," George recalled. "The judges said they would call Monday at 3:30 if I'd gotten it. I had to take a friend to the hospital that day, so I gave them the hospital number. As soon as the phone rang I knew what it was, because no one else had the number. Jack Lang told me and I was thrilled. He asked how I felt, but I couldn't tell him—a million things went through my mind, but I couldn't say anything.

"What felt best was my spiritual growth over the year. It was more important than the material gain." That's how George remembered the day he won the highest of baseball honors, the Most Valuable Player of the Year award.

He returned to Hawthorne to share his happiness with his family and friends. His mother still lived in the small yellow house George remembered so well,

UPI

*Hearing that he has been selected the National League's Most Valuable Player for 1977.*

but there was a difference. In front of the driveway the low chain link fence bore a new sign that read: "Visitors Please Park Outside."

Success hadn't changed him, but it had caused changes, and he and his family had to work hard at keeping his public and private lives separate. George didn't live there anymore, but when he returned home once or twice a year for the Reds-Dodgers games, his mother's house became a magnet for the old neighborhood. Everyone, black and white, from small children carrying ragged baseballs to old ladies wearing flowered hats, came to the house to visit George. Once in a while the group was treated to seeing George with friends Ken Griffey, Joe Morgan, Dan Driessen, or Davey Concepcion. The ballplayers were frank enough to admit they came not for George's company—they saw him all the time—but for his mother's wonderful chitlins, ribs, and corn bread.

Because of the award the crowd in front of the house was larger than usual. As George stepped outside to talk to the forty or fifty people standing in friendly groups, he noticed Rev. Austin Williams, his pastor from the True Vine Baptist Church, waiting for him with a van full of kids. Reverend Williams had helped George when he was lost and confused by reminding him to believe in himself, and George always visited him and the church when he was at home.

Because George believed that "not taking time to be with other people can be a person's downfall; we should be out there to help one another," he loved the crowd, even if it did take away some of his privacy.

He peeked into the van and immediately had several baseballs thrust at him. He signed them dutifully, and then his eye caught a little boy with an old baseball, its red seams almost split. The boy, too shy to push through the others to get the ball signed, just sat with the ball in his lap and looked at George. George held out his hand until the boy gained the courage to hand him the ball. George asked him his name and signed it with his tentative, unflourished signature. "I try to see how to reach different people," George would say. "With some it's a handshake, another an autograph, sometimes I tell them 'You're more important than you think.' " Always, though, George sought the child too small or too shy to ask for the autograph.

He left the van for a moment and returned carrying brand new baseballs and gleaming black bats which were Little League replicas of his own famous bat. The bats were inscribed in gold, reading "George Foster, Cincinnati Reds Slugger, 1977, National League, Most Valuable Player." The children eagerly took the bats and balls and jumped out of the van, looking for a place to play.

The following Sunday, the True Vine Baptist Church held George Foster Day, and the church was filled with old and new friends. First George spoke and thanked them for coming. A handsome figure in a finely tailored blue suit, George told them never to give up, to work hard, and most of all, to believe in themselves. They listened, because everyone knew George spoke from his own experience.

Then others spoke, sharing their affection and respect for the great slugger. One man said, "I knew him before he became a superstar and he hasn't changed any. As good an athlete as George is—and he's the best—he's a better man."

When the applause ended, Reverend Williams had the last word. "The only change in George now is in his confidence," he said. "George won the MVP award. To me that stands for the Most Valuable Person, because that's what he is."

People had come to see George Foster not only because he was a baseball star, but because he remained the good person he was when he left Hawthorne with only his dreams of being a big leaguer. One of the most respected players in baseball today, it isn't only his ability that other players admire, it is his character. As Pete Rose aptly put it, "George has more than average pride."

The year 1978 tested his pride as well as his patience, because the frustrating season mystified him. He wasn't slumping, but he wasn't getting the hitting streaks that marked the year before. Just when he thought that "things were coming into place," the feeling would slip away and he'd find himself struggling to find the groove again. A home run followed by a hitless game happened too often.

As the season wore on, he began to suspect that the problem was emotional. He'd played in pennant races before, but he never felt so much pressure not to let up. Once again the Dodgers were the team the Reds had to beat to prove they were better and to regain their position as world champions. Unlike the year before, the Reds stayed close to the Dodgers from the beginning, but they couldn't overtake them. When the Dodgers lost, the Reds lost, and when the Reds won, the Dodgers won as well.

No matter how hard the Reds tried, they couldn't jump ahead of the Dodgers because they were handicapped by injuries all year. Johnny Bench and Joe Morgan, two star players, were hurt and were played sparingly for the whole season. As Pete Rose said, "All clubs have injuries, but these are special cases. With Morgan hurt we lose our running game and with Bench hurt we can't control the opponent's running game."

Besides holding the Reds back, these injuries put extra pressure on the healthy players, especially Dan Driessen, Ken Griffey, and George. They felt driven to make up for the team's weakness. Sometimes an extraordinary effort works for a special series, but it's impossible to sustain for an entire season.

Although George's reputation still earned him more respect than any other hitter, after the All-Star game his average fell from the .300's into the low .280's. The special pressure of a division race that required keeping close despite injured players sapped too much of his energy. As George fell behind so did the team, and by the end of August Cincinnati's hopes for a division title ended.

There were other goals to keep George motivated, however. First of all, he wanted to keep the home run title he had earned the year before, and Philly left fielder Greg Luzinski hovered dangerously close. George's RBI title was precarious, too, because Pittsburgh Pirate Dave Parker had been on his heels all year, even passing him in September. George especially wanted the RBI title because he knew if he won it for the third straight year, he would be only the sixth man in history to achieve the feat. The last man to have won three straight times was Joe Medwick in 1938.

The year had been disappointing, but if he could hold onto the home run and RBI titles in the National League he would feel better about the year, and it would help make up for his .281 average. But by September 23 George had only thirty-five home runs and Dave Parker was hot as the Pirates made a late surge for the Eastern Division title. With only six games left, George needed a hitting streak to beat Parker and Luzinski, and that's exactly what happened. He hit five home runs, drove in ten runs, and hit .333 in the last week of the season.

The last game was against Atlanta on September 30 at Riverfront Stadium. Before the game, George prayed as he often did, this time thanking God for allowing him to play every day. By his fourth at bat he'd walked twice and was finding it hard to get a decent pitch. He fouled back two pitches, breathing easily each time the ball fell out of play. On the third pitch he swung hard and at the crack of the bat announced his 39th home run. It wasn't forty but it felt good, anyway. The Reds led 6–3.

Sparky Anderson wanted to take him out of the game after the homer to give the minor leaguers a chance to play, but George didn't want to leave. Although it was the eighth inning, there was always the possibility he would get another at bat. Just as he was about to ask Sparky to leave him in, he looked up into the stands and saw the fans giving him a standing ovation. After a year that hadn't been his best, their support was wonderful. The crowd convinced Sparky to let George finish the game.

George's wish came true, because when Atlanta rallied in the ninth to tie the score George got another chance. The two teams slugged it out until the fourteenth inning, when George came up to bat again. With his last at bat in 1978 he finished the season with his fortieth home run and won the game for the Reds 10–8.

By hitting his fortieth, he joined Boston Red Sox Jim Rice in being the only player to hit forty or more, won the home run title for his second straight year, and won the RBI title for the third consecutive time. With the RBI title he joined Hall of Famers Honus Wagner, Ty Cobb, Babe Ruth, Rogers Hornby, and Joe Medwick in the rare accomplishment of winning the title three times in a row. And finally, George succeeded in making one record all his own. In three years he had hit an unprecedented 121 home runs and 390 RBI's, more than any other currently active player had done in three consecutive seasons.

In his mother's house, George's room looks just the way it did when he left for the big leagues, except that the walls and shelves are filled with major league trophies and pictures. Three photographs in this collection stand out: Willie Mays, Roberto Clemente, and Henry Aaron. George calls them the Big Three and strives to be the fourth man. 1978, a year of grace under pressure, brought him much closer to joining their ranks.

# Statistics

| Year | Club | Pct. | G | AB | R | H | 2B | 3B | HR | RBI | BB | SO | SB |
|---|---|---|---|---|---|---|---|---|---|---|---|---|---|
| 1968 | Medford | .277 | 72 | 253 | 47 | 70 | 9 | 5 | 3 | 30 | 28 | 20 | 3 |
| 1969 | Fresno | .321 | 121 | 449 | 68 | 144 | 5 | 8 | 14 | 85 | 37 | 59 | 1 |
| 1969 | S. F. | .400 | 9 | 5 | 1 | 2 | 0 | 0 | 0 | 1 | 0 | 1 | 0 |
| 1970 | Phoenix | .308 | 114 | 403 | 54 | 124 | 18 | 6 | 8 | 66 | 41 | 57 | 1 |
| 1970 | S. F. | .316 | 9 | 19 | 2 | 6 | 1 | 1 | 1 | 4 | 2 | 5 | 0 |
| 1971 | S. F.-Cin. | .241 | 140 | 473 | 50 | 114 | 23 | 4 | 13 | 58 | 29 | 120 | 7 |
| 1972 | Cincinnati | .200 | 59 | 145 | 15 | 29 | 4 | 1 | 2 | 12 | 5 | 44 | 2 |
| 1973 | Indianapolis | .262 | 134 | 496 | 77 | 130 | 26 | 1 | 15 | 60 | 44 | 109 | 4 |
| 1973 | Cincinnati | .282 | 17 | 39 | 6 | 11 | 3 | 0 | 4 | 9 | 4 | 7 | 0 |
| 1974 | Cincinnati | .264 | 106 | 276 | 31 | 73 | 18 | 0 | 7 | 41 | 30 | 52 | 3 |
| 1975 | Cincinnati | .300 | 134 | 463 | 71 | 139 | 24 | 4 | 23 | 78 | 40 | 73 | 2 |
| 1976 | Cincinnati | .306 | 144 | 562 | 86 | 172 | 21 | 9 | 29 | 121 | 52 | 89 | 17 |
| 1977 | Cincinnati | .320 | 158 | 615 | 124 | 197 | 31 | 2 | 52 | 149 | 61 | 107 | 6 |
| 1978 | Cincinnati | .281 | 158 | 604 | 97 | 170 | 26 | 7 | 40 | 120 | 70 | 138 | 4 |
| **Major League Totals** | | **.285** | **934** | **3201** | **483** | **913** | **151** | **28** | **171** | **593** | **293** | **636** | **41** |

## Championship Series

| Year | Club | Pct. | G | AB | R | H | 2B | 3B | HR | RBI | BB | SO | SB |
|---|---|---|---|---|---|---|---|---|---|---|---|---|---|
| 1972 | Cincinnati | .000 | 1 | 0 | 1 | 0 | 0 | 0 | 0 | 0 | 0 | 0 | 0 |
| 1975 | Cincinnati | .364 | 3 | 11 | 3 | 4 | 0 | 0 | 0 | 0 | 1 | 2 | 1 |
| 1976 | Cincinnati | .167 | 3 | 12 | 2 | 2 | 0 | 0 | 2 | 4 | 0 | 4 | 0 |
| **Totals** | | **.261** | **7** | **23** | **6** | **6** | **0** | **0** | **2** | **4** | **1** | **6** | **1** |

## World Series

| Year | Club | Pct. | G | AB | R | H | 2B | 3B | HR | RBI | BB | SO | SB |
|---|---|---|---|---|---|---|---|---|---|---|---|---|---|
| 1972 | Cincinnati | .000 | 2 | 0 | 0 | 0 | 0 | 0 | 0 | 0 | 0 | 0 | 0 |
| 1975 | Cincinnati | .276 | 7 | 29 | 1 | 8 | 1 | 0 | 0 | 2 | 1 | 1 | 1 |
| 1976 | Cincinnati | .249 | 4 | 14 | 3 | 6 | 1 | 0 | 0 | 4 | 2 | 3 | 0 |
| **Totals** | | **.326** | **13** | **43** | **4** | **14** | **2** | **0** | **0** | **6** | **3** | **4** | **1** |

## All-Star Games

| Year | Club | Pct. | G | AB | R | H | 2B | 3B | HR | RBI | BB | SO | SB |
|---|---|---|---|---|---|---|---|---|---|---|---|---|---|
| 1976 | National | .333 | 1 | 3 | 1 | 1 | 0 | 0 | 1 | 3 | 0 | 0 | 0 |
| 1977 | National | .333 | 1 | 3 | 1 | 1 | 1 | 0 | 0 | 1 | 0 | 1 | 0 |
| **Totals** | | **.333** | **2** | **6** | **2** | **2** | **1** | **0** | **1** | **4** | **0** | **1** | **0** |

# Index